Homosexuality from the inside

an essay by

DAVID BLAMIRES

Published by the
Social Responsibility Council
of the
Religious Society of Friends
Friends House, Euston Road, London NW1 2BJ

Cover designed by John Blamires
Printed in Great Britain by Headley Brothers Ltd.,
109 Kingsway London WC2 6PX and Ashford Kent

Contents

Foreword

The Social Responsibility Council of the Society of Friends is glad to have facilitated the publication of this essay, written by an active and concerned member of the Society in collaboration with a small group, the majority of whom are also Quakers.

We welcome the opportunity of putting before Friends and others a sober and informed account of the position and feelings of some homosexual people in our midst.

It need hardly be added that an essay which is so clearly written on behalf of a minority group does not purport to represent the view of the Society of Friends as a whole nor of the Social Responsibility Council in particular.

However, this essay does represent both the spirit and the method in which we feel such a subject should be approached. In the first place it introduces candour to a subject where there is a history of concealment; and concealment, as we know, is a barrier to trust and thus to honest relationships between people. Secondly, as Friends who speak of 'that of God in every man', we are invited to try and understand the problems of those who may not feel or act as the majority do and to try to meet the difficulties that such a minority group encounters.

Friends are accustomed to the attempt to reach out in understanding to minority groups, sometimes to people who are fundamentally anti-social. In this instance we should remember that the homosexual minority amongst us often give, from deep conviction, most valuable service to our Society and to mankind at large. We should ask ourselves whether they might not be able to contribute more if the underlying fears, so clearly shown in this essay, could be removed.

We also record our sincere respect for David Blamires for putting his name to this essay; it is sad that this has to be labelled a courageous act.

We commend this essay for careful study, and as a basis for frank discussion. We believe that apart from its value in itself, it gives us all the opportunity to examine our own attitudes, whether of love, tolerance, antagonism or prejudice and through our examination of those attitudes the better to understand ourselves.

September 1972

CHRIS BARBER, *Chairman*
LESLIE A. SMITH, *Secretary*

Introduction

This essay has been written in the first place for members of the Society of Friends (Quakers). Those who have contributed towards its being written hope that it will help Friends to understand better the situation of that minority of people, usually estimated at about five per cent of the population, who are homosexual. Since homosexuals, both male and female, are found in all walks of life, it is likely that of the 20,000 Quakers in Great Britain about one thousand will be homosexual. This fact alone should make Friends consider what they are able to do for this substantial group of people if, like most others, they need help in their spiritual and emotional lives. The burden of guilt and repression which many may feel is a cause of great personal distress. It is not made any easier when some sections of the Christian community turn their backs on them unless they are prepared to suppress completely their affections for their own sex.

The homosexual—at least in the Western world—grows up into a society in which he feels he does not properly belong. Despite the considerable coverage which the media give to homosexuality in plays, films and news items, there are still very many people who do not realize at all clearly what it means to be a homosexual and yet function as an ordinary human being. Hence this essay. Although what follows has been written largely by one person, it represents the outcome of extensive discussion between homosexual and heterosexual Friends and others close to them. It has grown out of the concern of a small group of homosexual Friends that a new and responsible exposition might help to overcome some of the misunderstandings that are apparent. We hope that it may also

1

be of relevance outside the confines of Quakerism. The time has now come for society to make a positive move towards accepting the homosexual as a person with a pattern of experience that is as authentic as that of the heterosexual and that can be discussed and worked out with the same degree of rationality and understanding as is the case with the heterosexual.

This is not the first time that Friends have attempted to make a contribution towards a contemporary understanding of homosexuality. In February 1963 the Home Service Committee of the Religious Society of Friends in Great Britain published an essay by a group of eleven Friends called *Towards a Quaker View of Sex*. This eighty-four page book immediately attracted a great deal of publicity. It was the subject of a television programme. It was quoted and misquoted in almost all the daily newspapers, as much as anything because here a group of people, explicitly identified with a part of the Christian Church, was prepared, after several years of study, discussion and prayer, to put forward an approach to sexuality—and in particular homosexuality—that was radically different from what had hitherto been expected from a Christian body.

The authors of *Towards a Quaker View of Sex* started with a consideration of homosexuality because this was a specific matter on which their guidance had been sought. But the more they went into the question, the more they felt compelled to extend their investigation beyond this narrow section of the sexual spectrum. It may well have been this extension to sexual attitudes generally that caused disquiet among certain sections of the Society of Friends, but on the whole the publication of *Towards a Quaker View of Sex* was a liberation. It was widely read and discussed, perhaps less among Quakers than in society at large, and it is not an exaggeration to claim that it has played a significant part in the change of social attitudes towards homosexuality.

Towards a Quaker View of Sex expressed the kind of approach to sexual relationships towards which many people, especially among the younger generation, had been striving for a long time. It refused to pass simple traditional judgements on such matters as extramarital sexual intercourse or homosexual relationships. Instead, it asked searching questions about the depth and tenderness of relationships, about caring for other people, about wholeness and integrity and about the exploitation of other people for one's own satisfaction. 'Surely it is the nature and quality of a relationship that matters: one must not judge it by its outward appearance but by its inner worth. Homosexual affection can be as selfless as heterosexual affection, and therefore we cannot see that it is in some way morally worse' (*Towards a Quaker View of Sex*, p. 41). The authors were, quite rightly, not prepared to set up a precise moral code of what was permissible and what was not, but tried to provide a basis of judgement out of which the individual could develop an awareness of what was right in the particular situation in which he found himself. Its central chapter focussed on the issue of homosexuality, and there is a great deal of eminently good sense in what is written there.

Since 1963, however, there have been major changes in the law relating to homosexuality which have made certain sections of *Towards a Quaker View of Sex* out of date. With the Sexual Offences Act of 1967, homosexual relations between two consenting males over the age of 21 in private no longer constitute a criminal offence in England and Wales. This provision does not apply to Scotland or Northern Ireland, and homosexual acts are still illegal in the Armed Forces and the Merchant Navy. But although the Sexual Offences Act has brought about some change in the way in which homosexuals and homosexual behaviour are regarded by society at large, the peculiar situation in which the homosexual finds himself is still barely appreciated by the vast majority of heterosexuals.

One disability under which *Towards a Quaker View of Sex* labours is the fact that it was written largely 'from the outside', as was perhaps inevitable at the time when it was written. More than is the case now, homosexuality was then in large measure regarded as a 'problem', especially morally, but also socially and medically. It was then the particular province of doctors, lawyers and the Church to pronounce judgement, on behalf of society, on people who were never thought of as 'us' but always 'them'. The present study is, therefore, an attempt to remedy this lack in *Towards a Quaker View of Sex* and to provide some insight into what the homosexual himself or herself really feels and how differently the world looks from his or her particular angle. It is not an official Quaker view, but is intended as a contribution towards an ongoing discussion.

Attitudes Towards Homosexuality

When we speak as Friends of 'that of God in every man', we are asserting our conviction that the lives of all men and women have a spiritual dimension and that each individual has a place of inestimable value within the universe. Our individual capacities vary enormously. We cannot be 'all things to all men', but we must use the gifts we have to the best of our ability and help others to do the same. Human beings are capable of great things—courage, unselfishness, creativity, love —but we are also frail creatures and need support and affection in encountering the numerous problems of life. This applies especially in the area of sexuality and the emotions. If we confine ourselves here to the question of homosexuality, it is because homosexual men and women often have greater difficulties in establishing and maintaining sexual relationships at depth. It has long been our concern as Friends that every individual should have the opportunity to develop what is best in him. More could certainly be done by society to give homosexuals this opportunity. Personal relationships are important to all people, whatever their sexual orientation. Even more important is the fact that they should be caring and promote the growth of personality.

Since the homosexual grows up and lives his or her life in a society where many different attitudes towards homosexuality are found, it is perhaps advisable to discuss these attitudes first. They are a more or less constant concomitant to his own feelings and opinions and are thus important factors, sometimes positive, sometimes negative, in the search to understand his own identity.

Most of what has been written on the subject of homosexuality can be divided into three categories. There is, first of all, the confessional type of literature, written by homosexuals themselves and expressing their own subjective feelings. There is no need here to go into this further except to say that at most periods in which there is a flourishing literary tradition there are homosexual apologists and homosexual love poetry, ranging from Plato and Sappho to André Gide and Jean Genet, to mention only a few well-known examples. A second category consists of analytical studies, often produced by doctors, psychiatrists, lawyers and sociologists, who are interested in what they consider to be 'deviant' behaviour. Then, thirdly, there are the attacks on homosexuality from the point of view of a society or an individual that feels its values undermined by the very existence of homosexuals. The second and third of these categories need to be examined, if only briefly, for the contribution they have made to present attitudes.

The category of analytical literature on homosexuality is generally written by people of a tolerant disposition, though not universally so. This is the 'scientific' or pseudo-scientific literature on homosexuality. It varies immensely in quality and seriousness. Some of it is highly objectionable, misusing 'science' and statistics to bolster up obvious prejudice or ignorance. Some of it is highly articulate, intelligent and aimed at a real understanding of the homosexual situation. These are the studies which look at homosexuality and homosexuals from the biological, physiological, legal and sociological angles.

Those written from the medical and psychiatric or legal point of view tend to be concerned first and foremost with those few homosexuals who go to them or are referred to them because they are in distress. These people are either disturbed or mal-adjusted to their condition or they have come up against the law in the pursuit of satisfying their sexual desires. By and large, therefore, these studies generalize from the experience of

6

the disturbed homosexual to the experience of the homosexual in general. Since, however, the vast majority of homosexuals do not consult—and do not need to consult—a psychiatrist or psycho-analyst and do not get arraigned before the law courts (even with the laws slanted against them), the impression that this type of literature gives is necessarily one-sided. If it claims to speak, from this limited experience, about homosexuals in general, it is obviously false. One would not publish an article on marriage solely from the experience of a marriage guidance counsellor, nor would one begin to write about the nature of heterosexuality simply using material from prosecutions for rape or soliciting.

A further point needs to be made regarding much of the material treating homosexuality from the medical or psychological angle. This is the presupposition that homosexuality is either a disease or akin to a disease, whether psychological or biochemical. It is usually regarded as a deviation from the norm of heterosexuality (though there are a multitude of manifestations that heterosexuality can take too, some of them also frowned on by society) and not as a condition in its own right. Because *some* homosexuals are disturbed by their condition, it is often assumed that *no* homosexual could genuinely wish to be as he is and that he ought therefore to be 'cured'. It is all too often assumed that homosexuality in itself is the root problem of any homosexual in distress, but frequently the distress is caused by feelings of guilt at simply being what society disapproves of and by labouring under the constraints of such disapproval. In many other instances the fact of a person's being homosexual may be a complicating, but not necessarily radical, element in his troubles.

In the medical and psychological attention given to homosexuality considerable effort is devoted to 'curing' the homosexual from his condition and 'changing' him into a person with heterosexual desires. This kind of treatment can really only work where the person seeking help is uncertain about the direction of his sexual drive, that is to say, when he does not know whether he wants to be primarily attracted to his own or the other sex. But it cannot be assumed, even in such cases, that the person in question ought to be guided, as a matter of principle, into a heterosexual orientation. Each individual should be treated in the way that is more appropriate to his own personality and situation. He should be helped to realize what is truest to himself, to his own deepest needs as a person. The use of aversion therapy, whereby the homosexual patient is subjected to unpleasant sensations to make him reject his homosexual leanings and then given pleasant sensations with heterosexually biassed stimuli, should be rejected as a rule. There is no guarantee that it *can* change sexual orientation, and it may even do great psychological damage in making the person involved incapable of any sexual response. It is the violation of a personality justified on grounds of conformity to a heterosexual norm falsely held to be valid for all and sundry.

This study is *not* concerned with the possible causes of the homosexual condition. This is a field on which much has been written, but in which little has emerged in the way of undisputed facts, although there appears to be a general consensus that homosexuality is not to be regarded as a congenital condition, but arises through various environmental factors. The trouble with most of the research on the causes of homosexuality is that it ignores or underestimates the existential aspect of homosexual experience. It fails to do justice to the fact that the main problem the homosexual comes up against is society's reaction towards his natural behaviour and emotions. The anxiety that his condition may cause him is largely the result of his attempt to accommodate to society's demands and in the process to deny his own nature. This produces guilt not

8

only in the homosexual, but also in the homosexual's family. It is foolish to assert that homosexuality is the result of 'faulty upbringing' and to produce the conventional stereotypes of weak or absent father and dominant or possessive mother (in the case of the male homosexual). This grotesque over-simplification (at best) is generally of no positive help to the homosexual himself, and it may produce an intolerable feeling of guilt in the parents too.

The behaviour and psychology of individuals who belong to minority groups is, of course, of copious interest both to members of such a group and to people outside it. Very many homosexuals are fascinated by the question of what made them what they are, and the case-histories that usually form a sub-stantial part of books on homosexuality are often the most readable sections. These histories, however, are so varied that it is virtually impossible to isolate a common cause or basis for homosexuality. In any case, the assumption underlying such studies, whether it is explicit or concealed, is—to put it crudely —that homosexuality is a condition society would be better off without; if its roots could be understood, it could perhaps be eradicated.

If these studies do not go so far as to state, for example, that homosexuality is a physiological disturbance which could be corrected by hormone treatment, or a psychological state which psychotherapy or drugs could alter or control, or an immature phase out of which the person involved should be assisted to develop, they may very well take the view that 'homosexuality is a condition to be pitied rather than con-demned'. One would certainly not wish people to condemn, but for them to pity is also something which would cause many homosexuals embarrassment. To consider homosexuality as a weakness of the flesh to which a number of poor unfortunates are prone is an attitude to be found in the pharisaical—'thank

9

God that I am not as other men are'. Such condescension is destructive of the integrity of all concerned. Certainly give help and sympathy where it is asked for, but there is no need to think of anyone as deserving of pity simply for the fact of being homosexual. That there are problems to being homosexual is not to be disputed, but these are more realistically to be considered as resulting from the fact that homosexuals are a minority group.

In turning to the third category of outlook on homosexuality —the condemnatory one—the Christian homosexual is confronted with a hard problem since he finds the condemnatory view firmly rooted in the Old Testament and taken over from there in the New Testament and much of the succeeding Christian tradition. It is, however, not a view which is argued in any detail, but is simply set out as if there could be no argument about it. No specific reason is given for the condemnation. The whole matter has been examined from the historical angle in a careful study by Derrick Sherwin Bailey, *Homosexuality and the Western Christian Tradition* (London, etc. 1955), where the Biblical passages mentioning homosexual practices are judiciously analysed. From the brevity of these statements and the omission of any reasoned arguments to support them, it is difficult to discuss them. It has been argued that the prohibitions of the Mosaic Law are related to the necessity for the Israelites of that period to maintain their identity as a separate people and to propound a distinctive moral outlook. Beyond this, Rabbinic tradition has regarded homosexual acts as frustrating the procreative purpose of sex and damaging the basis of family life (see, for example, the article on Homosexuality in the *Encyclopaedia Judaica* (Jerusalem, 1971)). The Mosaic Law, however, was formulated in and for a type of society vastly different from our own and can hardly be taken as normative for the twentieth century.

10

The New Testament has very little more to say about homo-sexuality, and it is all contained in the letters of Paul. In writing to the Christians at Corinth he says: 'Surely you know that the unjust will never come into possession of the kingdom of God. Make no mistake: no fornicator or idolater, none who are guilty either of adultery or of homosexual perversion, no thieves or grabbers or drunkards or slanderers or swindlers, will possess the kingdom of God' (1 Corinthians, vi, 9-10). In the letter to the Romans he speaks of the wicked who have turned away from God and says: 'For this reason God has given them up to the vileness of their own desires, and the con-sequent degradation of their bodies, because they have bartered away the true God for a false one, and have offered reverence and worship to created things instead of to the Creator, who is blessed for ever; amen. In consequence, I say, God has given them up to shameful passions. Their women have exchanged natural intercourse for unnatural, and their men in turn, giving up natural relations with women, burn with lust for one another; males behave indecently with males, and are paid in their own persons the fitting wage of such per-versions' (i, 24-7).

In neither of these two passages is Paul attempting to discuss the morality or otherwise of homosexuality as a human condi-tion. As Bailey suggests, his statements are to be interpreted as 'the Christian reaction to the dissolute sexual behaviour of the Hellenistic world, which was regarded as the inevitable con-comitant of idolatry' (*op. cit.*, p. 60). What seems to have out-raged Paul particularly was lust, i.e. sexual acts devoid of the genuinely personal element, but he accepts the Old Testament view on homosexuality without modification. However, since his remarks on homosexuality are merely incidental to his main theme, they do not offer an adequate point of departure for further discussion.

11

In the Biblical point of view there appears to be no problem in determining what is 'natural' and what 'unnatural'. The condemnation which homosexual acts receive—and sodomy is the one on which attention mainly focusses—seems to be based on the idea that the female is essentially subordinate or inferior to the male and that if a male has sexual relations with another male this constitutes an act of degradation since it involves treating a male as an inferior being (see Bailey, *op. cit.*, p. 162). The Christian Church, at least until recently, followed the line of approach of the Old and New Testaments, regarding all homosexual acts as a 'perversion' from a uniform heterosexual condition. It did not recognize, any more than any other section of society, the nature of homosexuality as a human condition. Although this is now generally accepted, some sections of the Church still maintain that all homosexual acts are sinful *per se* and that the only way a homosexual can be pleasing to God is by making a sincere effort to sublimate his sexual desires.

Many people who condemn homosexuality—or more properly, homosexual acts—base their opposition on the danger that they consider it represents to the family. They tend to regard the sexual instinct as primarily, if not exclusively, related to the propagation of the species. In this context, homosexual relations, like extramarital sex or sexual intercourse using contraceptives or between people too old to have children or physically incapable of having children, represent a threat to an oversimplified view of the purpose of human sexuality. The elements of pleasure and desire, which may be satisfied without the intention of producing a child, cannot easily be fitted into a view of this kind. Such acts are often characterized as being 'irresponsible' or 'immature', but this sort of attitude towards them fails to do justice to the diverse manifestations of sexuality in human life. It is based on what

12

seems to be a distorted view of the nature of human experience. The strengthening and deepening of personal relationships which sexual intercourse, at its best, does bring, aside from any intention or possibility of producing a child, ought never to be undervalued. Indeed, this deepening of relationships lies at the heart of sexual experience, and without it the raising of children would be a task of daunting proportions.

Some of the antagonism felt by heterosexuals towards homosexuality is related to ignorance of their own psychological make-up. Most heterosexual women have no anxiety about homosexual men; indeed, they often get on very well together because they can have a relationship uncomplicated by sexual factors. Some heterosexual men, however, feel threatened by the homosexual woman, who competes with him on his own ground, unaffected by his sexual charms. But both heterosexual men and women may experience some obscure uncertainty (to put it at its lowest) with regard to homosexuals of their own sex, if they are not stable in their own personal relationships or are not fully conscious of the range of their own psychology or secure in their own sexual identity. In some cases this uncertainty derives from guilt feelings about what it is 'right' or 'proper' to feel and desire. If one experiences in oneself desires categorized as 'wrong' or 'improper' in one's own upbringing, it is not unlikely that one will project this fear of oneself on to another person who exemplifies it. It may be also that guilt feelings about adolescent homosexual experiences thought of as 'dirty' make it hard for one to accept homosexual behaviour in an adult.

Furthermore, the basically heterosexual person may wonder, consciously or unconsciously, what might happen to him emotionally if he were to give expression to homosexual feelings. Would he become a different sort of person? Would it upset or interfere with his basic heterosexual inclination?

13

Such anxieties are real ones and ought not lightly to be dismissed, but one argument of this essay is that very many individuals are capable of a wider range of emotional and sexual responses than they think and that such responses are not to be rejected out-of-hand or frowned upon as 'unnatural'. This does not mean that everyone should or will jump into bed with anybody else at the first available opportunity—there is in any case an enormous variety of expression for emotional attraction between individuals—but that people should be encouraged to develop their emotional natures and stop repressing their feelings which are, in the right place, perfectly positive and enriching. Homosexual emotions are not a symptom of a disordered personality: they are as real and good as heterosexual emotions. They are not in themselves more attractive or less attractive than heterosexual feelings. It is absurd to think that homosexuality is more powerful than heterosexuality and that its pleasures are such as to lead the heterosexual to abandon his normal state.

Sexual Roles and Orientation

To what extent is the sexual orientation of the individual a matter that is open to change? The sexual spectrum may be looked at in at least three ways. One may see, first of all, a variety of sexual experience ranging from that of the heterosexual, who is exclusively attracted to the opposite sex, through the bisexual, who is capable of responding to either male or female, to the homosexual, whose emotions are directed only to his or her own sex. There is, secondly, the entire question of what constitutes masculinity or femininity in the individual human being. Is any person completely male or female to the exclusion of the other? Thirdly, there is the question of the individual's psychological development, in which homosexual experience may or may not play a part.

It is perhaps this last question that provides the strongest argument for doctors and psychiatrists in treating homosexuals as people needing to be assisted on the path to heterosexuality, for very many of them do think of homosexuality as an adolescent 'phase' of development beyond which some people, for whatever reason, do not progress. This whole matter is complicated by the fact that many males and females who in adult life are unambiguously heterosexual have experienced homosexual attachments in adolescence. The 'crushes' that teenage girls frequently have on an older girl or mistress at their school are a commonplace of life and are accepted by society, generally with a degree of amusement, but sometimes with annoyance or embarrassment. Adolescent boys often go through similar experiences. Since the physical side of sex tends to be much more to the fore in the male than in the female, this may very well be simply a physical thing without any deep-seated emotional component. This is illustrated, for example, in Brian Aldiss's novel *The Handreared Boy*, where the scenes of mutual masturbation are reserved for those boys for whom one has no particular affection or respect. Nonetheless, romantic attachments between teenage boys are not uncommon either and may very well represent one of the most intense experiences of boys who grow up into 'normal', well-adjusted heterosexual men.

The fact that many men and women go through a period in which they experience homosexual emotions need not imply that those for whom this is their *only* experience are in some way 'immature' or, even worse, 'sick'. It is a basic presupposition of this essay that there are very many people for whom homosexuality is as 'normal' and ought to be as acceptable as heterosexuality is for the majority of human beings. The same goes for bisexuals, who may well fall into the awkward position of being viewed with suspicion or disfavour by both heterosexuals and homosexuals alike. It may well be that what society thinks of as adolescent homosexuality is, more accurately, a manifestation of bisexuality, which in many people is blocked out in adult life through the pressures exerted by society.

The question of what constitutes masculinity and femininity is one that is hard to answer. Even on the simply physiological plane there are some people, admittedly not very many, whose sex is difficult to determine and who have severe problems in establishing their sexual identity. There are then also people whose physiological sex is clear, but who, at least to some degree, identify themselves emotionally with the other sex and like to dress in the clothes appropriate to the other sex. Apart from this, there are certain physical characteristics which tend to be considered 'masculine' or 'feminine', and where, for example, the tone of voice or the growth of facial hair does not correspond to the statistical norm, the person in question may

16

be thought to be 'effeminate' or 'mannish'. Human beings exhibit an extraordinary variety in their physical appearance and behaviour.

More important is how different societies, races or tribes categorize masculinity and femininity according to personality traits and social function. Certainly, as far as social function is concerned, what one form of society may consider to be proper behaviour for the male or the female may be thought quite out of place in another.

The matter of social roles is one that is currently under attack in Western society, as the growth of the Women's Liberation movement plainly shows. The purely domestic, male-dependent role of the female is being challenged on all sides, though there are still very few men who would be willing to take on the main part in bringing up small children and looking after the home while their wives went out to work. The role of 'mother' and 'housewife' is in fact so well-defined and ingrained that a man who exhibits similar patterns of behaviour is liable to be viewed with grave suspicion if his parental instincts receive any expression outside the bounds of his own family.

A nasty illustration of such prejudice is to be found in the fate of the American teacher, Gerhard Braun, whose fatherly instincts in showing affection to his pupils provoked the false accusation of child-molesting. Although at the trial which ensued he was declared innocent of all the thirty-eight charges trumped up against him, he was forced to leave the area in which he had been living and his teaching career was ruined (see the article by Robert Blair Kaiser, 'What happened to a teacher who touched kids?' *Look* Magazine, 10 August 1971). This is not directly concerned with the issue of homosexuality —Gerhard Braun was not a homosexual—but it exemplifies the extraordinary reactions of some sections of Western society when a person steps even a little outside the rigid conventions of society.

The expression of affection or emotion by men is severely restricted in northern Europe and America, and those who try to break through the barrier of the touch taboo are liable to find themselves in difficulties of many kinds. The expression of emotion in crying, whether through pain or sadness, or in kissing in order to show affection or sympathy is thought to be a 'feminine' characteristic and thus to be avoided by men. Conversely, the woman who tends to take the initiative in actions or relationships is often held to exhibit 'masculine' traits, to be thought of as dominant, if not domineering, and thus also to be exceeding what is expected of her as a woman. However, it is now becoming more usual to accept that every human being possesses both male and female characteristics to some degree and that it is natural, for example, for men to have feelings of tenderness towards others, and that this may or may not have a sexual element in it. One of the main aims of both Women's Liberation and Gay Liberation is to persuade society at large that the range of human emotion and experience is such that a much greater degree of flexibility is needed in our ideas about what constitutes masculinity and femininity.

When it comes to considering the relationship of homosexuality, heterosexuality and bisexuality to each other, one should beware of trying to identify homosexual men as 'feminine' or homosexual women as 'masculine'. It just doesn't work on that basis. Homosexuals are as varied in their physical and emotional natures as all other human beings. One certainly cannot deduce on the basis of physical appearance whether a person is likely to be homosexual, except perhaps in the case of some people who correspond closely to the stereotype of homosexuality with which society is familiar, that is, the conventionally effeminate man, ever concerned with his appearance, or the conventionally mannish woman, who may tend to dress as much like a man as possible (which, incidentally, is far more acceptable in the eyes of the world than the man who wants to dress like a woman). The average homosexual man or woman looks like anybody else from his or her particular walk of life.

Immediately one begins to talk about the 'homosexual' or 'homosexuals' one is confronted with problems of generalization. Possibly the only thing one can say about all homosexuals without fear of being contradicted is that they have a primary sexual and emotional attraction towards their own sex. Apart from this, homosexuals are as varied in character, temperament and behaviour as any other human beings. As Michael Launder says: 'No one uses the word "heterosexual" to describe another person (except in the presence of a homosexual). Yet the label "homosexual" is used time and time again, often accompanied by a knowing wink, as if it conjured up a whole personality and way of life. For example, to say that Hitler was a heterosexual means absolutely nothing, but just imply that he was homosexual and a large number of people will believe that they have discovered the reason for the Second World War' (see *Forum*, vol. 4, no. 11, p. 12.)

What we need to remember is that people are individuals. We are all searching, some perhaps more dimly and hesitantly than others, for meaning in life, and each of us will find it in a way peculiar to our own situation and experience. In certain respects the homosexual does function in a different way from the heterosexual and does have different attitudes, but in many ways he will have similar viewpoints and engage in similar activities to his heterosexual neighbours, colleagues, relatives and friends. In fact, where he is primarily identified as simply another human being—sexual likes and dislikes being irrelevant—the homosexual will be accepted without question or thought. It is only when or where he is identified primarily as a homosexual and thus neatly categorized so that stock responses can be made to him, that difficulties arise, both for himself and for others. The average homosexual does not want to be known as 'a homosexual', but as a person who, among other things, happens to have as one element in his make-up a sexual and emotional preference for his own sex. The rest of this essay will attempt to indicate the range of homosexual experience while concentrating on those areas that might be said to constitute the 'middle ground'.

The Pressures of Society

Before going on to discuss the pressures under which most homosexuals live, we need to look briefly at the particular situation of female homosexuals. Although both male and female homosexuals are characterized by a primary sexual attraction to their own sex, it cannot be assumed without further qualification that statements which are generally valid for male homosexuals will also be valid for females. In the United Kingdom lesbians have not, for example, suffered the penalties of the law in the pursuit of fulfilling their sexuality. Social pressures, however, can be just as destructive of human relationships and well-being as the more clearly formulated sanctions of the law. Indeed, some would be prepared to argue that the discriminations of the law have provided a rallying point for male homosexuals, focussing objections and strengthening the will to get things changed, whereas the undefinable nature of society's disapproval, in the case of lesbians, is a much more difficult matter to contend with. Ridicule, malicious gossip and ostracism, wherever they occur, are unpleasant and wounding. Their effects may be more lasting than a prison sentence. But society's failure to take female homosexuality as seriously as male homosexuality—there is far less information about it readily available—is also damaging to the lesbian's image of herself and her self-respect.

There are, of course, some differences in the attitudes of male and female homosexuals. There tends to be a greater degree of defensiveness among lesbians as opposed to the occasional flamboyance of the male homosexual. For the male the physical side of sex tends to assume a greater importance, where for the female it is the emotional component that is to the fore. This is not to say that men are incapable of deep emotional involvement, but rather to emphasize that with women sexual relationships are much more closely bound up with feelings. Apart from this, however, there are large areas where one can speak with a fair degree of confidence for most homosexuals, whether male or female. Hence what follows is relevant to both.

The homosexual lives the greater part of his or her life in an alien society. It is a world in which the tune is called by the heterosexual male. It is one where *his* sexual preferences, *his* fantasies even, permeate almost every aspect of life. In this world, male-female sexual relationships are assumed to be universal. Advertising is probably the most obvious manifestation of this assumption. The pretty girl, the 'dolly bird', figures in every possible place, whether the product sold is really connected with her or not. It scarcely matters whether the aim is to sell chocolate or cigarettes, a car, a camera or a kitchen sink, the picture of a sexually attractive woman makes it sell. In this world the role of the female is seen as essentially dependent on the male. She has virtually no claim to existence in her own right. Much the same is true of the world of entertainment— the theatre, films, television, newspapers and magazines. This sexual gratification of the heterosexual male is so much taken for granted that some readers of this paragraph will almost instinctively reject the view put forward here or regard it as quite exaggerated. Nonetheless, it has more than a grain of truth in it, and this is how the world appears in the eyes of very many homosexuals.

Perhaps a further example may illustrate the difference in attitudes. A girl who gets whistled at down the street is assumed to enjoy the compliment. No heterosexual man would think it necessary to suppress his reaction to the sight of a girl he found attractive, except perhaps if he were with another girl who might find his admiration irritating. If he is out with his wife

22

or girl-friend, he can express his affection for her as he wishes. He can hold her hand, look lovingly in her eyes, kiss her, hug her, and do any number of other little things. A few people will think he could be less demonstrative in public, but by and large no one will brand his behaviour as 'indecent'. More probably, people will think his actions touching and regard him at worst with mild amusement. As the saying goes, 'all the world loves a lover'.

But not all the world loves the homosexual lover, though his or her emotions are every whit as real as those of the hetero-sexual. Our society seems as yet unable to accept the reality of homosexual love and affection, and the homosexual is thus forced to conceal or damp down his true feelings in public. If he does attempt to express his feelings in public, he is likely to be jeered at or insulted. He is not able spontaneously to wel-come his lover or friend with a kiss at a railway station, but has to wait until they get to the privacy of home to express his delight. The pleasure of dancing together has to be reserved for a club or a private party, and in the case of clubs there is quite a real risk that the police may intervene and bring a charge. Such arbitrarily imposed restrictions on behaviour are hardly conducive to the true growth of personality. Where true emotions of this kind cannot be freely expressed, the indi-vidual's powers of feeling and sense of involvement with the lives of other people will become stunted or split off from other aspects of his life. Indeed, because of this taboo on tenderness between males especially, many homosexuals do in fact lead split lives. With their 'gay' friends, they are one kind of person; in 'straight' society they are another.

The examples of restrictions given above may perhaps seem trivial, but they are in fact symptomatic of a more fundamental alienation that the homosexual experiences, and it is with this that we are concerned. Unfortunately, the average man and woman just do not realize the kind of emotional anaesthesia to which homosexuals are condemned, until this is plainly pointed out to them. They may be able to accept the 'camp' behaviour of the theatre or the stunning drag-shows of Danny La Rue, but this is because what is otherwise thought of as extravagant, eccentric or flamboyant is perfectly all right in the context of the theatre. It is rendered harmless because it takes place 'somewhere else', in a setting which is not part of ordinary, everyday life, but insulated from it. But once such patterns of behaviour are brought into the sphere of the day-to-day, they may appear as a threat to the security of the predominantly heterosexual world.

It is occasionally asserted that the life-style of the homosexual undermines the family and is a threat to the security and the welfare of adolescents. It cannot be denied that the more radical wing of the Gay Liberation Front views the nuclear family, in its present social manifestation, as an oppressive unit. As their manifesto puts it: 'It is because of the patriarchal family that reforms are not enough. Freedom for gay people will never be permanently won until everyone is freed from sexist role-playing and the straight-jacket of sexist rules about our sexuality. And we will not be freed from these so long as each succeeding generation is brought up in the same old sexist way as the patriarchal family' (*Gay Liberation Front Manifesto*, London, 1971, p. 9). This may seem an alarming and aggressively formulated view to many people, but it is one that is shared by other non-homosexual groups and not simply the section of society represented by the Gay Liberation Front. It is part of the widespread revolt against the rigid stereotypes of what it constitutes to be male or female. Of course, in so far as family life is open, flexible and accepting of the diverse ways of being human, the average homosexual will have no particular desire to upset it.

There is nothing inherently more attractive about homosexuality that would cause any heterosexual person to wish to abandon his normal sexual mode, unless he should happen not to be completely heterosexual in the first place. People do not give up a life-style lightly, even though they may experience considerable difficulties within it. Many people who in later life are unambiguously heterosexual may, especially in their adolescent years, experiment with an occasional homosexual experience, but a single experience of such a kind is hardly likely to make any difference to basic sexual orientation. A person is not made into a homosexual simply by the performance of one, or even several, acts with another person of the same sex. Similarly, and this needs to be emphasized, a homosexual can't be made 'straight' through being subjected to a heterosexual pattern. This is a fact which very many heterosexuals seem unable to understand.

The situation with regard to adolescents is more complicated. Here again, it is amazing how many heterosexuals seem to think that any homosexual, simply by virtue of being homosexual, is likely to molest children. The offence of child-molesting is one which involves a tiny number of both heterosexual and homosexual men. In neither case has it anything to do with the condition of heterosexuality or homosexuality as such, but it is a social problem of its own kind. It is a widely held view among those with knowledge of the working of the law that the damage done to minors in a sexual assault can easily be exaggerated. The subsequent experience in the court may well be much more traumatic and give the assault a disturbing emotional significance that is hard to overcome.

In our society it is virtually impossible to discuss the matter of sexual relationships between men and boys in a rational spirit; it is a question which arouses the strongest emotions.By and large, the lover of boys or pederast is thought to be a particular menace, but the problem lies in deciding the age up to which the law should protect a boy from the sexual attentions of an older male. There is a difference between a child and an adolescent, and again between an adolescent and a man. According to the provisions of the Sexual Offences Act a male needs to be 21 before he may engage in homosexual acts with another male in private, yet the age of majority is 18 and at that age he is considered an adult. For a female on the other hand, the age of consent is 16. Society does not become disturbed or very emotional if a 50-year-old man marries a 17-year-old girl. However, if a 50-year-old man were to have a sexual relationship with a 17-year-old boy, society would put the man in prison, judge that the man had corrupted the boy and sit back in righteous indignation, paying little or no attention to any other considerations. The matter of mutual consent could not be used as a legal defence. But relationships between adults and adolescents on the sexual plane do not all fit neatly into the conventionally assumed pattern of seduction of the adolescent by the adult. There are clearly also situations in which some adolescents may actively desire to engage in such relationships because they fulfil their basic sexual needs. At this point the question of responsibility for actions becomes acute, and many people will prefer to judge that the adolescent's responses are not to be trusted or encouraged. Exploitation is, obviously, to be condemned in any relationship, but it ought not to be assumed that this is necessarily a factor in every relationship between an adult and an adolescent. However, it should be stressed that the relationship between homosexuals is one based on the love of a person of one's own sex and *not* on love between the old and the young.

With regard to the age of consent, the law relating to homosexual acts is far from being on an equal plane with that applied to heterosexual acts. At present there is some discussion about lowering the age of consent for both boys and girls from 16 to 14. A Quaker conference held at Oxford in April 1972 under the auspices of the Penal Affairs Committee advocated a uniform age of consent of 14 for both males and females, whatever the nature of their sexual relationships.* This position was also taken up by Dr. John Robinson, Chairman of the Sexual Law Reform Society, in an address to the Methodist Conference in July 1972. It is important here to recognize that this recommendation was in neither case conceived as an encouragement to such sexual relationships, but rather to prevent persons under the present age of consent from being liable to criminal law proceedings and to allow doctors and counsellors to help them without running the danger of being accused of aiding and abetting a criminal offence.

Against such a lowering of the age of consent for male homosexuals, it might be argued that since boys reach puberty and mature sexually and emotionally somewhat later than girls, it would be preferable to have a higher age of consent. Behind this argument there seems to lie the assumption that homosexual acts as such are undesirable and that any adolescent engaging in them is liable, if basically heterosexual, to become corrupted by them. Since, however, a large proportion of conventionally heterosexual males appear to have passed unscathed through a phase of adolescent homosexuality, it seems hardly likely that a reduction in the age of consent would result in an increased incidence of homosexual behaviour generally. It would simply remove the danger of criminal proceedings being taken against those persons who *of their own free will* engage in such acts. The emphasis here should be placed on the voluntary aspect of such behaviour, and any sexual activity involving force, coercion or any real lack of consent would rightly continue to be a criminal offence.

* The Penal Affairs Committee itself favours a minimum age of 15.

27

The Process of Self-Discovery

The idea that a person may be influenced or persuaded into being a homosexual is one that dies hard. Some people perhaps have a real choice of life-style because they are bisexual, but the majority of those who ultimately identify themselves as homosexuals do not have a choice in the matter. It is simply a question of *when* they recognize that their sexual interest is directed towards members of their own sex and come to terms with it. Some people, because of the strong pressures that society and family exert against them, never consciously accept their homosexuality and thus live with constantly unresolved tensions within them. Others come to the realization sooner or later, and there may be very considerable differences in the time-scale. Some people are aware of their homosexual inclinations from childhood onwards, and for them it is a matter of amazement that others do not discover the fact of their homosexuality until perhaps their early twenties or even later. Probably males are more conscious of their desires in this respect than females. The pressures on females to marry and have a family are much stronger than those on the male to do the same, and because the conventional role of the female to respond to male initiative and be dependent on him is much better developed, there are many women who only find out after marriage and in middle life that they are in fact homosexual. Possibly a majority of lesbians have tried out the heterosexual pattern of life and found it unsatisfactory.

Given the current attitudes of society, a person's discovery of his homosexuality is liable to be fraught with anxiety and complications. It must be a rare experience for a young person to be able to share with his parents or siblings the fact that he has fallen in love with a member of his own sex and to do this with openness and confidence that his news will not shatter them. Much more frequently one's initial experiences will be tentative, hesitant and secretive experiences to keep to oneself. Since practically everything that one will have come across in the way of references to homosexuality will be in terms of a condition that applies to 'somebody else', one may have difficulty in recognizing one's own feelings to be natural or acceptable. It may be a long process of self-discovery, involving some preliminary attempts to reject what one has found, before one can accept the reality of one's situation and learn to love. There may also be a considerable gap between accepting that one is emotionally attracted to one's own sex and actually engaging in an explicitly sexual relationship. Because of the inhibitions and prohibitions set up by our Western society it may be extremely difficult for some people ever to bridge this gap. There are probably large numbers of older people, both men and women, who have repressed their real feelings to such an extent and for so long that a re-orientation is virtually impossible. No matter how much such a person may realize his position in intellectual terms and wish to overcome it, the legacy of repression is hard to conquer.

The process of self-acceptance in the homosexual is usually lengthy, but sharing the fact that one is homosexual with others is an even lengthier process. It is a rare person, who, in the present climate of society, is able to express the fact of being homosexual in a completely natural, matter-of-fact way in the ordinary course of events, without suppressing any reactions that he really feels. Much of the reluctance to express one's situation arises from the common heterosexual assumption that homosexuals have a fixation on sexual activity, in other words that to be a homosexual is equivalent to engaging in sexual acts rather than to having a primary emotional attraction to persons of one's own sex. Moreover, the general oppressiveness of society makes the average homosexual cautious as to whom he decides to tell about himself. There is almost always a fear of the possible rejection he may experience.

However, at some point or other, many (perhaps most) homosexuals feel a definite need to tell at least some of their heterosexual friends about themselves, because the concealment of this aspect of their character works against the growth of understanding and friendship, and because the lies involved become too much to bear. It represents an act of incalculable trust, and like all acts of trust it may evoke a response of acceptance or it may result in a breakdown or cooling-off in the relationship. It is not an easy situation, and when the reaction to one's act of trust consists of some degree of rejection, one has lost out on the matter. It may be, of course, that the friend to whom one has thus revealed oneself is embarrassed or anxious lest he should become the focus of one's sexual affections, but this is a genuine life-situation and has to be coped with in the same sort of way as other inter-personal relationships in which people make impossible demands on each other. Some people may only be able to solve this by complete withdrawal, as in the case of a male-female relationship which has broken up after a time of sexual involvement and which cannot be replaced by a non-sexual friendship.

Possibly the most emotionally exacting self-revelation for the homosexual is that regarding his or her parents. It is a situation which perhaps the majority refuse to contemplate, believing that it would serve no useful purpose, but would simply cause unnecessary anxiety. Given the present attitudes of society, it is likely that many parents would indulge in painful self-recriminations, asking themselves repeatedly 'Where have we gone wrong that this should happen to us?' This kind of reaction grasps the information given as a judgement of themselves and largely ignores the situation of their offspring. It flourishes on the theory of homosexuality as a 'sickness' or 'psychological immaturity' and allows great scope to the parents' feelings of self-centredness and desire for control over their offspring's lives. Some other parents accept the situation superficially, but go on to a virtual refusal to speak further about it, preferring simply to exclude it from everyday conversation as if they had never known anything about it. This is almost as unpleasant an experience as that of straightforward rejection. Indeed, it makes homosexuality into the literally 'unmentionable' topic. Many parents are, of course, willing to accept their offspring's homosexuality as regards their own family relationship with him, but they may not want this to be public or widespread knowledge, fearing the reactions of their neighbours, friends and colleagues. The parents who can fully accept their offspring's homosexuality, neither trying to conceal it, nor seeking to flaunt it, but speaking naturally about it as the occasion demands, are a rare phenomenon indeed.

When it comes to the question of speaking of homosexuality with regard to one's colleagues, the majority of homosexuals will prefer to keep silent. If they are in public employment, they will be prudent to do so since the prejudices of society are liable to make themselves felt with devastating effect. There seems to be what amounts to a virtually pathological fear on the part of parents, for example, that a homosexual teacher will corrupt the children in his care through simply being known to be a homosexual. Similarly the homosexual clergyman may often be thought to be unworthy of carrying out his Christian duties and responsibilities. Public knowledge that he is homosexual will be liable to negative every practical and spiritual gift he may have. Moreover, if any person in political or governmental life is 'exposed' as a homosexual, he is likely to be ejected from his position and hounded from public usefulness.

The unreasonableness of this view is obvious when one realizes that so long as a person's homosexual nature remains unknown, his service to society will be accepted on the same basis as anyone else's. The fact that he is a homosexual makes no difference to the performance of his duties, since it is totally irrelevant to the job he has to do. Yet most homosexuals justifiably regard it as politic to keep silent about this aspect of their personality where their career is concerned, such is the discrimination that the heterosexual majority exercises. When the Gay Liberation Front aligns itself with the oppressed sections of society, with non-whites who are discriminated against in employment, housing and public service, and with women who are exploited for their cheap labour, there is some reason for their action. But for a homosexual to obtain redress for wrongful dismissal from employment, he would have to face publicity of a kind that might be extremely distasteful to him personally. Rather than have his private life exposed to possible mockery and vilification, he will probably put up with the injustice perpetrated against him. In his public life and career the homosexual is therefore more or less compelled into patterns of behaviour in which caution, discretion, and some-times downright dishonesty towards himself are required. There must be many homosexual men who adopt the attitudes of heterosexuals in regard to women and who find it helpful to be seen with or talk about women friends from time to time in order not to arouse the suspicions of their colleagues and workmates. Some even go so far as to enter into marriges of convenience in order to camouflage themselves. Homosexual women may also have to cope with the attentions of hetero-sexual men who find them attractive and thus cause embarrass-ment and difficulties.

The Formation of Relationships

When all is said and done, the average homosexual wishes to do nothing other than lead a life in which he can be as useful to society as the heterosexual and to be allowed the same latitude in his sexual behaviour as the heterosexual. He suffers, however, in the first place from the great disadvantage that since society from childhood onwards is geared to the needs and desires of the heterosexual he will find it difficult to know where his own needs and desires may be satisfied. The chances of the homosexual finding a sexual partner through the ordinary channels of social activity are immensely smaller than those of the heterosexual, though the proliferation of marriage bureaux and advertisements in the personal columns of many magazines and newspapers indicate that the heterosexual also has problems in finding a partner. Yet just at this point where one might imagine that a well-worded personal advertisement would provide a helpful means for like-minded persons to meet each other, the homosexual may find himself in difficulties with the law, as the case brought against the *International Times* amply demonstrated.

IT had a personal column in which some small advertisements were placed for homosexuals to contact each other. According to one of the Directors, the intention 'was to provide in good faith a public service for a minority of individuals who had been continually discriminated against, harassed and victimized. As a newspaper with some sort of social conscience we thought we could make a positive and practical contribution to the welfare of homosexuals'. These advertisements attracted the attention of the police, and the publishers of *IT* were fined £1,500 after being found guilty of the rare Common Law offences of conspiring to corrupt public morals and conspiring to outrage public decency. The defendants appealed against the decision but at the final appeal to the House of Lords the sentences were confirmed on the first count, but set aside in the second. This thus countenances the extraordinary state of affairs whereby advertisements are held to be corrupting morals even though the acts envisaged by them—i.e. sexual behaviour between consenting male adults in private—are not a crime. In the House of Lords it was claimed that there is 'a material difference between merely exempting certain conduct from criminal penalties and making it lawful in the full sense' (see *The Times* law report, 15 June 1972). This is only one example of the general situation in which homosexuals find the law in practice used against them, where similar conduct on the part of heterosexuals is not regarded as actionable.

Because of the difficulty of meeting other homosexuals in the ordinary way of things and on account of society's disapproval of overtly homosexual behaviour in public, many male homosexuals gravitate to places where they are more likely to find other similar people, i.e. gay bars and clubs, to some steam and sauna baths, to certain areas of parks and beaches, to public lavatories. Generally speaking, these areas will not be frequented by heterosexuals, or only rarely so, and so the homosexuals will be able to strike up acquaintance with each other in the multifarious ways that are open to all human beings. Behaviour will range from the most ordinary, innocuous conversation to complete sexual gratification, depending of course upon the surroundings and desires of the individuals involved. For many homosexuals, both male and female, to be in a gay bar or club, where they can be themselves without the need for 'covering up' or pretence at being something different from what they are, is a liberation.

Nonetheless, as the National Council for Civil Liberties

Guide points out, the police are entitled to exercise their discretion in carrying out their duty of preserving the peace and they may disrupt homosexual parties or close down clubs, if the people present are not behaving like heterosexuals. 'In September 1968, the Manchester magistrates fined a club owner for having allowed men to dance together. Evidence was given by the police who had visited the place in plain clothes that it was "a haunt of homosexuals". Presumably the homosexuals themselves were not outraged by single-sex dancing. Nevertheless, the owner pleaded guilty to having permitted dancing of a nature likely to cause a breach of the peace' (*Civil Liberty: The NCCL Guide*, edited by Anna Coote and Lawrence Grant (London, 1972), p. 166, quoting from Antony Grey, 'Homosexuals: New Law but no New Deal', first published in *New Society*). All of this illustrates the area of uncertainty within which homosexuals have to make personal relationships. It is hardly surprising that they make proportionately fewer stable relationships than heterosexuals.

In addition to meeting in bars or clubs, some homosexual men use public lavatories for sexual purposes. However, if research done in the United States is any guide to the British situation, it would appear that the majority of men (some 54 per cent) involved in this kind of impersonal sexual encounter are married and living with their wives, but find that some of their sexual needs are not met by them (see Laud Humphreys, *Tearoom Trade* (London, 1970)). The element of risk or adventure often plays a positive part in 'cottaging' (as it is referred to in British slang usage). It adds to the sexual excitement of the men involved and may indeed be an essential part of their enterprise. These encounters are generally without commitment, anonymous, brief and, from the viewpoint of the ordinary person, easy to condemn. They are clearly unattractive and offensive to many people, but the offensiveness

35

is more in the idea than in the reality of the act committed.

Because of the difficulties of meeting other people who start from roughly the same presuppositions, both male and female homosexuals often suffer from an acute sense of isolation. Anybody who belongs to a minority group, whether religious, political, racial or social, will know how important it is to have that group for support when the rest of the time one lives one's life among people who do not share the same interests or aims. This must be within the experience of very many Friends. It is for similar reasons that homosexuals seek out gay bars and clubs, etc., because here they know that their particular outlook on life will be shared. People who raise their voices in protest against homosexuals seeking out each other's company and living a 'ghetto existence' ought to remember this fact. In this kind of situation it is virtually inevitable that the emphasis will be on meeting someone else with a view to sexual activity, and usually sooner rather than later. The whole set-up tends to be predatory and promiscuous and to inhibit normal opportunities for the gradual growth of a relationship. It is a rather hit-and-miss business, but when one considers the rare chances of meeting, in the ordinary way of things, with another person who may respond to one's sexual interest in him, it is a situation that one is well-nigh forced to accept. There are, however, many homosexuals who do not find their way to gay bars and the like—perhaps because they do not know how to find them, because they are too shy to approach others in this way, perhaps because they just do not like the situation and are prepared to accept the deprivation of sexual relationships that this may entail.

By and large the homosexual finds his or her sexual partners in the reverse fashion to that by which boy meets girl or man meets woman. Heterosexuals will generally meet their partners on a basis of some shared interests and a similar outlook on life. The expression of their sexual feelings for each other will grow naturally out of this and out of their developing affection for each other. The homosexual, on the other hand, cannot afford to assume that a person he meets in the ordinary course of events and to whom he feels attracted in terms of shared interests or friendship will respond in the slightest degree to him in sexual terms. Indeed, he may very well find himself emotionally involved with heterosexual individuals who are totally unconscious of his involvement with them. Thus, the likelihood that a homosexual will meet his life partner on the basis of non-sexual interests is very small. He is more or less forced into the opposite approach. The sexual interest comes first. Only when a mutual sexual attraction exists—it does not need to have been translated into physical terms—is there a point in exploring further areas of interest and attitudes towards life. Often, however, the relationship may never proceed further than the sexual stage; this is where the relationship *begins* rather than being the culmination of an experience of growing together.

If our society accepted the homosexual as simply another human being and homosexuality as another style of sexual preference, without making any value-judgements, it is possible that more homosexuals would wish to adopt, as a norm, a similar pattern of long-term pairing to that of heterosexuals. More or less every individual, whether homosexual or heterosexual, hopes to find some other human being with whom to share his life. For the average heterosexual this is usually within his compass, though the number of divorces, separations and marriages in name only make one realize that a stable, life-long or long-term relationship is not to be taken for granted by anybody. For the ordinary homosexual a stable relationship is something that, in many cases, he hopes against hope for.

37

There are, indeed, homosexual couples who succeed in living unobtrusive, happy lives together, remaining faithful to their partners in the manner expected of ordinary heterosexual couples. That many more homosexuals desire, but cannot achieve, such permanent relationships is also clear. Some would like to think it possible that there might be homosexual marriages in the sense that their relationship could be publicly declared and legally recognized. For some it would be important to add to that a religious aspect; they would want the opportunity for a homosexual couple—if we may think of it in Quaker terms—to express their commitment to each other in Meeting and ask for the support and blessing of the Meeting on their life-long partnership.

There are, of course, many implications and problems arising from any idea of homosexual marriage and this is not the place to go into them. The important point is to appreciate that even to talk in these terms is evidence of the wish of many homosexuals for longer-term stable relationships. These are very much hindered by the present attitudes of society, and until a major change takes place a pattern of transient relationships may be the unavoidable lot of the homosexual and, in particular, he may have to face, especially in looking forward to old age, the prospect of that loneliness that the absence of permanent or family relationships implies.

To the extent, then, that current social attitudes do not help to foster and sustain permanent relationships, homosexuals who desire sexual activity—obviously a normal thing to want—may feel compelled into a series of casual contacts. A person whose sexual behaviour is characterized as 'promiscuous', whether male or female, heterosexual or homosexual, is generally thought of as irresponsible in his attitudes towards others, incapable of any deep or lasting feeling, and merely out for swift self-gratification. But this is not necessarily and

38

universally the case, and indeed those whose sexual relationships are casual may have been forced to split off their sexual
needs from other areas of their life, simply because they have
not found it possible to achieve anything any other way. But
there is no need to assume that they are *ipso facto* insensitive
or unfeeling to individuals. There is a price to be paid for
everything in life, and the price of insulating their sexual
desires from everything else may be the one they have decided
to pay.

It is well known that men, whether heterosexual or homosexual, are much more quickly and easily stimulated to sexual
desire and activity than women. Their reactions are closer to
the surface of their being, they respond more swiftly to touch,
their sexual emotions may be aroused quickly and certainly
subside more quickly after orgasm than women's emotions.
Men may, thus, often not be *emotionally* involved in their
sexual encounters. They may in fact be content with the simple
physical satisfaction of their sexual urges and look elsewhere
for their emotional needs or for companionship. This is not a
state of affairs that is confined to homosexual men, but has its
counterpart among heterosexual men, including those who are
married. The purely sexual instinct, which varies a great deal
in intensity from person to person (a fact every individual needs
to keep in mind), may therefore be satisfied through a series of
partners. The kind of relationship involved may range from
an anonymous sexual act over and done with in a matter of
minutes to a physical expression of tenderness and concern
between two people who have struck up a real, if nonetheless
brief, regard for each other. Some of the readers of this essay
will, no doubt, be disgusted that *some* male homosexuals
apparently desire nothing more than straightforward relief
from sexual tension. It is clear, however, that such people are
settling for what can actually be obtained rather than aiming

at an ideal of mutual involvement and caring which may be totally beyond their reach.

It is important in the discussion of most subjects to try to understand them in their own terms. Much of the trouble with discussing homosexuality arises from the fact that it so often tends to be talked about in terms that derive from and are only comprehensible with reference to heterosexuality. Many heterosexuals, for example, fix their curiosity on such matters as who is the 'male' and who the 'female' in a homosexual relationship, thus transferring their own conception of sexual roles to a situation which is, at least initially, not transparent to them. Of course, the idea of more or less pre-determined sexual roles is in the process of being modified among heterosexuals nowadays, but many of them nonetheless apply the traditional concept to homosexuals too. Probably among some older homosexuals there are elements of role-playing, but among the younger generation the idea of 'male' and 'female' is pretty well irrelevant. There are, obviously, differences in temperament between homosexual partners, as there are between heterosexual partners, but such differences are matters of personality rather than of sexual role. The conventional stereotypes of 'butch' and 'bitch' or 'femme', 'active' and 'passive', are favoured by people who are more interested in pigeon-holing and type-casting than in the subtle complexities of real human behaviour. What is important is that people should demonstrate their affection and make love as creatively as possible, bringing pleasure and delight to each other in the ways they find appropriate at the time. Adaptability and concern for the well-being of one's partner, together with truth to oneself, are of the essence of any two-way relationship. They are no easier for the homosexual to attain than for the heterosexual.

There is a need for radical changes in social attitudes so as to enable homosexuals to see themselves as normal people and to to be and act in ways that are natural to them. In the sphere of sex education also changes are called for. In concentrating on the heterosexual ninety-five per cent, most books tend to lose sight of the homosexual teenager, who is liable to come away from reading them with the feeling that he has been cheated. His own particular emotions and problems may not even be dealt with, or they may be treated in a totally inadequate or dismissive way. The subject is certainly complicated by the fact that many adolescents who later become well-adjusted hetero-sexuals do experience homosexual emotions too. But it still needs to be pointed out that for some adolescents, albeit a minority of them, homosexual emotions are and will continue to be their only and normal experience.

There are, unfortunately, very few books on sex education that touch on the subject of homosexuality at all helpfully, as one recent analysis of the literature tries to show (see Maurice Hill and Michael Lloyd-Jones, *Sex Education. The Erroneous Zone*, National Secular Society, 1970, pp. 20-3). Too often the result of sex education is the production of guilt in the ado-lescent, largely because of unresolved conflicts in the educators, who are simply reproducing the conflicts of attitudes in society at large. This kind of attitude is to be noted in those people who declare that homosexual emotions are 'all right', but that it is better for them not to be physically expressed. There are, unfortunately, some people who seem to believe that if one is homosexual one ought to lead a life from which all physical sex is banished, even in adulthood. This is not a view that the collaborators in this essay find defensible. The prejudices and prohibitions with which sex has been hedged about in our society need to be removed and more positive, realistic values put in their place. Given the centuries of repressive attitudes towards virtually all sexual activity in the

West, including marriage, it will be no easy matter to achieve a more balanced view that does justice to the observable facts of sexual experience.

Conclusion

This essay has tried to show that homosexual emotions are just as real and good as heterosexual emotions and that they are not to be regarded as symptomatic of a disordered personality. The homosexual has, however, problems of self-discovery and of forming relationships in a society that is, in an important sense, alien to him or her. There is clearly a need for radical changes in social attitudes so that homosexuals may see themselves as normal people and be accepted as such by society at large. It would help a great deal if more homosexuals were courageous enough to identify themselves, in the appropriate circumstances, so that people could recognize that among their friends and neighbours, relatives and colleagues, there are many ordinary, inconspicuous individuals who happen, among other aspects of their personality, to be homosexual. Changes in matters of law are certainly necessary, but much more important are changes in the general attitudes of society. Above all there is need for the openness and candour that could come from an honest recognition of homosexuality as one element in the total make-up of society. Such acceptance of the truth and respect for individuals, whatever their sexual orientation, are surely matters that will commend themselves to the serious consideration of Friends.

Further Readings

The literature on homosexuality in books and articles is immense. The list that follows offers simply a very brief selection of books that chime in with the viewpoint expressed in this essay.

Dennis Altman, *Homosexual Oppression and Liberation* London: Angus & Robertson, 1973.

Derrick Sherwin Bailey, *Homosexuality and the Western Christian Tradition* (London: Longmans Green, 1955).

Brian Magee, *One in Twenty* (London: Secker & Warburg, 1966).

Norman Pittenger, *Time for Consent* (London: SCM Press, 1970; second, revised and enlarged edition, 1971).

Charlotte Wolff, *Love between Women* (London: Duckworth, 1971).

Addresses

The following organizations are all concerned with promoting the welfare of homosexuals and assisting them, where necessary, with any problems.

Albany Trust, 32 Shaftesbury Avenue, London, W.1.

(Mainly concerned with research and education, but also acts as a referral agency; does not do any counselling work itself.)

Arena 3, BCM/Seahorse, London, W.C.1.

(Women only; both social and educational; produces a magazine for lesbians.)

Campaign for Homosexual Equality, 28 Kennedy Street, Manchester M2 4BG.

(Comprehensive, middle-of-the-road organization, involved in a broad range of social, educational and political activities; produces a monthly bulletin for members; groups in many parts of the country.)

Gay Liberation Front, 5 Caledonian Road, London, N.1.

(More militant and left-wing than the Campaign for Homosexual Equality; both social and political in its aims; produces magazines and pamphlets; attracts attention through publicity-conscious action; groups in several large towns.)

Kenric, BM/Kenric, London, W.C.1.

(Women only; exists basically for social purposes.)

National Federation of Homophile Associations, 65 Shoot-up Hill, London, N.W.2.

(Provides liaison between the various organizations working in the field.)

Scottish Minorities Group, 214 Clyde Street, Glasgow, C.1.

(Very similar in aims and outlook to the Campaign for Homosexual Equality, but principally active in Scotland.)